FOUNDATIONS OF MUSIC EDUCATION SERIES
Allen P. Britton, Editor

Singing

in the

Elementary Schools

PRENTICE-HALL INTERNATIONAL, INC., *London*
PRENTICE-HALL OF AUSTRALIA, PTY. LTD., *Sydney*
PRENTICE-HALL OF CANADA, LTD., *Toronto*
PRENTICE-HALL OF INDIA (PRIVATE) LTD., *New Delhi*
PRENTICE-HALL OF JAPAN, INC., *Tokyo*

Singing

in the

Elementary Schools

HARRIET NORDHOLM

Chairman, Department Music Education
Professor, Elementary and Music Education
University of Miami
Coral Gables, Florida

PRENTICE-HALL, INC., *Englewood Cliffs, New Jersey*

Foreword

The practical aim of the Foundations of Music Education Series is to provide music educators with a unified but highly flexible and completely authoritative treatment of the most important professional concerns. Individual books of the series may be combined in various ways to form complete textbooks for the wide variety of courses in music education offered by colleges and universities across the nation. On the other hand, each volume has been designed to stand alone as a definitive treatment of its particular subject area.

The pedagogical aim of the series is to present practical and proven techniques of successful teaching in compact and readable form for both college students preparing to teach and experienced teachers constantly searching for more efficient ways of thinking and teaching. The highest musical ideals must be accompanied by the greatest amount of practical common sense if music instruction is to be most successful.

The aesthetic aim of the series is to emphasize the purely musical values that must be realized in any program of music instruction if that program is to achieve ends worthy of the time and effort required to carry it on. In short, each of these works assumes first of all that music must be true to itself if it is to continue to hold a respected place in American education. The most telling criticisms made of the school music program in recent years, almost all of which have dealt largely with alleged aesthetic failings, have written this lesson in letters large enough for all to read.

Last, having pointed out the unifying concepts that underlie the works in this series, it is perhaps equally important to emphasize that each of the authors has written the book that he wanted to write, the book that he believed would be of most value to the profession. The series encompasses the individual convictions of a great variety of the most highly competent and experienced music educators. On their behalf as well as on my own, may I express the hope that it will contribute in a practical way to the improvement of music teaching.

ALLEN P. BRITTON,
EDITOR

Preface

Music has a variety of meanings. It says different things to different people. It is thought of, practiced, talked about, evaluated in dozens of ways. In whatever manner it is approached, however, the result should be the child's positive feelings of warmth and pleasure in music. creativity

It is well to remember that each child is potentially musical. Believing that, it becomes the dedicated responsibility of the teacher to help the child find his musical niche so that music may become an important facet of his life. While some benefits may be gained from developing a program designed only to entertain and afford pleasure, those qualities in and by themselves bring few lasting values. There must be depth and breadth in the program; there is need to educate so that each child may grow and develop to his own potential level of musical achievement. There is so much to be accomplished in a limited amount of time that every opportunity must be utilized and every circumstance seized upon to weave music into the life of every child.

Music should not be dealt with in isolation, but in its setting of human life and experience. It should be used spontaneously and naturally as a part of daily living. Music is neither an intellectual pastime nor a display of technical acrobatics. It is an experience important to every human being and his culture.

Harriet Nordholm

Contents

Singing

in the

Elementary Schools

1

Why?

Singing cannot be considered in complete isolation to the other areas of music. Moving, listening, playing, creating, *and* singing each interweave with one another into a fused totality. It is quite impossible to divorce one activity from the other; indeed, each depends upon the other in varying degrees. However, because singing is basic to the total music education program, and because the voice is so intimately associated with its owner, the teacher must prepare himself most carefully to conduct this aspect of the program.

A child singing spontaneously, enthusiastically, wholeheartedly has found one activity to bring him a fulfillment which nothing else in the curriculum can do. Singing is something that belongs *exclusively* to him. It is a skill he will use today, tomorrow, and for the rest of his life—in a variety of settings.

There is no way to measure the tensions that are released nor the moods that can be expressed when a child sings. With a good teacher and in a proper atmosphere, every youngster will soon learn that his singing voice is always available for him to use in his own way. He will soon discover, also, that there are many ways to produce music. Once having made such a discovery, he will have found his musical niche and be ready to approach music with a warm, at-home, joyous feeling. There can be no negative attitudes of apathy or even distaste if his early experiences in singing are to be success-ful, or, more important, if his musical growth is to move ahead as it should.

Susan, a six-year old, was asked by an adult if she liked music. She replied, "I like all kinds of music except what we have in school." When such an attitude is prevalent to even a small degree, there is something drastically amiss in the music program. In this instance there was nothing wrong with Susan, and there is cer-tainly nothing wrong with music, but there was something very much wrong with the combination of the two.

Every teacher must evaluate his music program honestly and critically in terms of what is happening, through music, to each child in his charge. Should there be even one Susan in his group, every effort should be made to reconstruct goals and procedures, to create positive situations, and to use those materials which will bring forth changed attitudes toward music. The Susan to whom we refer happened to be in a situation where there was only one objective: to "read notes." This objective is important, as shall be seen presently, but only as a part of the entire program, not as the sole activity. To make every child fit into a restricted role is disaster. He must be recognized as an individual and must be permitted to approach music in his own way. If he is to sing well, he must like to sing and want to try it for himself. He must feel free as an indi-vidual and as part of a group to sing spontaneously. With this kind of freedom, then and only then can he, through a song, express his feelings, attitudes, emotions, intellect, and understanding. The at-mosphere *must* be relaxed.

The singing aspect of the total music program should have only one focus—the child. Is he growing and developing through the songs he sings? How does he feel about those songs? His attitude toward singing is dependent upon two factors: (1) the song itself, and (2) classroom climate. He must be led into activities that immediately engage his talents so that he will feel successful and fulfilled. Perhaps the following chapters will serve to illustrate various ways these sometimes unrealistic-sounding goals can in-deed be accomplished.

2

What?

CHOICE OF SONGS

The songs actually sung in class constitute the crux of the entire question of whether children like to sing or not. It is imperative that each teacher appraise with utmost care the songs he asks the children to sing and the songs they, in turn, choose to sing. To maintain balance, songs from all historical periods and of all types should be sung. The text and the music itself should be of interest to children of a given age.

The child should be given opportunities to understand and evaluate in his own terms all kinds of songs. He must be helped to understand that each kind of song can have value. It is extremely difficult to attempt to define "good" music or "bad" music or "worthwhile" music or music with "little value." Nevertheless, the teacher, dedicated to his art, must lead the child to set his *own* high standards; his taste is usually reliable. He will instinctively react positively to songs that say something to him, to songs with which he can immediately become involved. A child's potential is often underestimated. He can only rise as high as his teacher will take him and there is no ceiling on where he can go.

Because curricula are becoming more crowded and complex, it is only the ingenious teacher who can find time for a well-balanced program. Since there are time limitations for music also, it is absolutely essential that whatever time is available be spent in the best possible way, remembering that, essentially, schools are not in the entertainment business. The teacher must, first of all, broaden his own repertory, enliven his own interest, develop his own enthusiasm for all kinds of music. If he, the teacher, loves opera, chances are his students will also love opera; if he is a symphony enthusiast, his students will catch his boundless enthusiasm, take it unto themselves, and become devotees of this art form also. If a teacher is eager to try new things, to experiment with "different," interesting sounds, the children will go right along with him. The teacher cannot give something which he does not have.

To broaden, enrich and enliven the repertory, these types of songs should be included:

1. Folk songs which sing of times, places, and situations to which children easily relate.

    The original composer, usually not known, was a creative music personality. He expressed his innermost feelings in a song. Others, hearing it, repeated it, added to it; someone at some point recorded it, and thus the song came to be.

    a. Western (hemisphere) folk music from diverse ethnic groups and geographical locations.

    b. Non-Western (hemisphere) folk and tribal music.

2. Art songs that encompass the children's interest and activities.

    Usually one person, an artist-composer, is responsible for the art song.

    a. Western classics from all periods, early to contemporary.

    b. Non-Western classics from all periods, with special emphasis on contemporary composers.

3. Spirituals, Negro and white, that may tell about history, wars, fears, hopes, beliefs.

4. Songs for special occasions, events, holidays.
   Assembly "sings," using songs from this or other categories are very worthwhile.
5. Songs that point up a specific classroom situation.
   a. Having read a story about Western expansion, sing a song such as "Goodbye Ol' Paint."

GOODBYE OL' PAINT

Traditional Cowboy Song

Good - bye ol' Paint I'm a leav - in' Cheyen - ne Good

bye ol' Paint I'm a leav - in' Cheyen - ne.

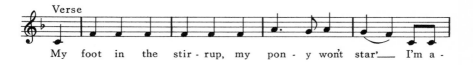

My foot in the stir - rup, my pon - y won't star'__ I'm a -

leav - in' Cheyen - ne an I'm off for Mon - tan'.__

b. Space travel is being discussed; sing "In Our Rocket."

IN OUR ROCKET

Words and Music by Ruth De Cesare

We will rock-et to the moon some day, And catch a

star as it pas - ses while we're flash - ing by.

When our rock-et's read- y and our course is stead - y

we'll see a new world some where in the sky.

Used by permission of Ruth De Cesare, copyright owner.

     c. It is raining; sing "Rain," or some other suitable song.

RAIN

Words by Robert Louis Stevenson
Music by Mary Beck Stevens

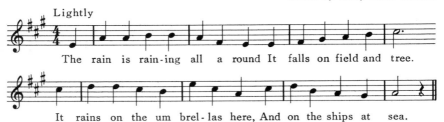

Lightly

The rain is rain-ing all a round It falls on field and tree.

It rains on the um brel - las here, And on the ships at sea.

From *Growing With Music*, Book 3, p. 64. © 1963 by Prentice-Hall, Inc.

6. Songs composed by children.
7. Songs that have to do with everything and nothing.

     Many times a song is taught and sung not because it represents anything concrete but because it is beautiful or lively or relaxing or stimulating or silly or serious!

In selecting songs, the teacher should keep these factors in mind:
1. Is the song one which the children will enjoy singing repeatedly; or, having been tried once, will it soon be forgotten?
2. Has the song been composed with exact craftsmanship, or was it simply put together to exemplify technical problems?
3. Is there a totality of all of the elements of music present, each integrating with the other, or does just one element predominate?
4. Does the song bring forth feelings and attitudes that cannot be expressed in any other way except by singing?

Songs have certain characteristics that should be evaluated in establishing criteria for selection:
1. Melody
   If the musical ideas are imaginative and provocative, ranges may be extreme. This is the range in which young children sing most comfortably:

C to D or E

2. Rhythm
   Complex rhythms with interesting variations and developments offer no great difficulty if they capture the child's interest. As a matter of fact, they prove less troublesome, usually, than the more regular, simple rhythmic patterns.
3. Harmony
   Songs with complex harmonies that invoke interest, surprise, and satisfaction are appealing to children. They enjoy songs where descants, counter-melodies, drone bass, or chord roots may be added. Songs harmonized in thirds and sixths are always good.
4. Form
   There should be repetition and contrast, movement and

rest, tension and release, unity and variety. These patterns should be heard, felt, and seen. Children should explore and discover simple binary and ternary form. Analyze such a song as "Drink to Me Only With Thine Eyes" something like this:

	Phrase Grouping	Structural Grouping
"Drink to me only with thine eyes,	A	
And I will pledge with mine,		Question
Or leave a kiss within the cup,	A	
And I'll not ask for wine.		
The thirst that from the soul doth rise,	B	
Doth ask a drink divine,		Answer
But might I of Jove's nectar sup,	A	
I would not change for thine."		

5. Expression

Songs should convey to the performer and to the listener feelings of tone color, mood, tempo, dynamics.

There are other characteristics to consider in choosing songs:

1. Repetition

Some of this is essential; too much makes a song uninteresting.
2. Variety

a. If a group is over-stimulated, a song such as "Cradle Song" would immediately change the restive mood to one of quietness and tranquility.

CRADLE SONG

Words by H. R. Wilson
Music by Franz Schubert

Slum - ber, slum - ber,   ten - der   lit - tle__ flow - er   Moth-er's lov-ing care

doth a - round thee twine. Sweet and rest - ful be___ this hour,___

Sooth - ing fall___ this lull - a - by___of___mine.

From *Growing With Music*, Book 3, p. 64. © 1963 by Prentice-Hall, Inc.

b. If the children are lethargic, "Funiculi, Funicula" can help to bring zest back to the classroom.

FUNICULI, FUNICULA

Neapolitan Song by Luigi Denza

Some think_____ the world is made for fun and frol - ic___
Some think_____ it well to be all mel - an - chol - ic___

___ And so do I,_____ And so do I!_____
___ To pine and sigh_____ To pine and sigh_____

But I_____ I love to spend my time in sing - ing___

___ Some joy - ous song_____ some joy - ous song___

___ To set_____ the air with mus - ic brave - ly ring - ing___

___ Is far from wrong,_____ is far from wrong!___

Refrain

Hark - en!   Hark - en!   Mus - ic sounds a - far!

Hark - en,   Hark - en,   Mus - ic sounds a - far Fun - ic - u -

li   fun-ic - u - la - fun-ic - u - li - fu-nic - u - la!

Joy   is ev - ry where fun-ic - u - li,   fun-ic - u - la!

c. When children have been sitting still for a long period of time, it is wise to have them sing while they stand and stretch: "Ev'rybody Stand Up."

EV'RYBODY STAND UP

Pennsylvania Folk Song
Adapted by H. N.

Ev 'ry bo - dy stand up   stand up, stand up,   Ev ry bo - dy stand up,

just like   me,   Ev 'ry bo - dy stretch high stretch high   stretch high

Ev 'ry bo- dy stretch high, Just like me.

d. When there are some talkative children, get the group singing "All Night, All Day" and the talking will cease!

ALL NIGHT, ALL DAY

Spiritual

All   night,   all _____ day,   Ang - els

watch- ing ov - er   me, my   Lord __   All   night,

all _____ day, Ang - els watch- ing ov - er   me. _____

In the use of folk materials, it is strongly recommended that authentic music from every part of the world be included. It is most
desirable that foreign songs be taught in their original language.
Children enjoy them, learn them easily, and are truly enthusiastic
over acquiring linguistic skills through texts from foreign songs.
Translations, at best, often lose authenticity, validity, and local color.
Teachers sometimes avoid songs from the Orient, for example, which
at first glance appear to be difficult and even formidable. Children,
however, accept and enjoy these new, exotic sounds. They will,
moreover, have more interest, understanding and knowledge of
people everywhere by singing such songs. A valid correlation occurs
when one sings not *about* Indians but, rather, sings the native
Indian song in an authentic setting.

Children should be encouraged to compose their own songs. Doing so involves them, enchants them, and permits them to express themselves as nothing else can. Making up tunes is a marvelous motivation for the study of theory. Once a child knows there are certain things he must know to notate his songs, he will be willing and even anxious to learn those specifics This is. another example of learning being significant when there is a felt need for it. Once songs have been composed, they should be sung frequently during the music period. Such songs should be shared from room to room in the school, in the city, or even in the state. An exchange of children's songs throughout the country would be delightful.

There are things to avoid in choosing songs:

1. Songs are sometimes composed for certain specific purposes, usually for teaching some facet of theory. Almost always such songs are inferior.
2. Themes from symphonies or other master works have been arranged into songs—often with inane words, where too many liberties have been taken with the composer's original work. There are many quality songs available without using these questionable, synthetic materials.
3. Songs which children simply do not like.

At one time advice was given to primary teachers indicating that young singers should be taught very short, simple songs. Such a practice is no longer followed for, as a matter of fact, children of all ages will learn songs that interest them regardless of difficulty or length. Neither is it wise to say that part-singing must be reserved for older children, because quite often six-year olds sing harmony charmingly and accurately. It is, in fact, extremely difficult, if not impossible, to prescribe what song shall be sung when. Only the teacher who knows her group can accurately make a judgment on this. Generally speaking, it is perhaps better to stretch children's capacities by giving them songs that may appear to be too difficult than to stifle them with materials too simple or not sufficiently sophisticated to satisfy their needs.

This idea goes along with the philosophy in general education to eliminate grade levels as such. Rather than organizing schools on a grade-by-grade basis the plan increasingly used is one of a lower school–upper school or a primary grades–upper grades kind of organization. The implication here for the music program is that the children sing a song, not necessarily because it is from a second-grade book, but because it satisfies the needs and desires of boys and girls regardless of their ages or grade levels.

3

When?

There is no one best time to sing; any time is a good time. Most teachers like to have a specified period set aside for daily music experiences. This is good. State departments of education usually require that there be a twenty or a twenty-five minute music block each day. That also is good, but there is no requirement stating that music be taught at the same time each day and always in periods of a given number of minutes. On some days there may be five minutes here, five minutes there, and ten minutes at another time; or, if interest is high on a particular day, the teacher might continue for 45 minutes. The next day there might be only a few minutes of music. The important thing is to seize every opportunity at any time to make music more meaningful for boys and girls.

In these days of accelerated mathematics, science, and language programs, some educators feel that music in the curriculum is in a precarious position, and, indeed, wonder if it will survive. It can and will, if its impact on children is strongly positive. What Johnny says about music at home is the best advertisement the program can have, if his attitude is positive.

Several years ago in a large, metropolitan school system, all eighth-grade general music classes were abandoned in favor of science and mathematics. Within a year these classes were reinstated. By whom? Not initially by school administrators or the board of education, but by the children themselves whose vociferous voices reached their parents, whose even more vociferous voices reached the proper authorities!

Some people, in their zeal to make boys and girls proficient in scientific considerations, have overlooked the fact that, above everything else, a child must be a human being. Recently, a Dean of a School of Education said, in reply to clamoring voices raised for more hours of mathematics and sciences and fewer hours for the arts, "When we take that trip to the moon, wouldn't it be pleasant to sing a song while getting there?" This statement seems simple, but a basic truth pervades: What a person *feels* about what he knows may be more important than that which he actually *knows*.

4

How?

LEARNING TO SING

A child learns to sing in much the same way he learns to speak. He hears people about him talking, and he talks; he hears people about him singing, and he sings. This urge to "make a joyful noise" must be nurtured and developed. Every effort a child makes to sing should be encouraged and praised, never quelled because he is not "singing in tune."

Children are sometimes self-conscious about using their voices and are usually most reluctant to sing alone. This need not be. Some of the following devices for young children may release them from these feelings:

1. Encourage children to sing individually during "telling time." They will happily learn from this activity that they can sing their ideas as easily as they can speak them.

    "David, would you like to sing about the new shoes you are wearing?"

He may sing a tune like this:

David:

See   my   new   shoes,   they're   shin - y   brown.

"Joan, how would you like to sing about the new baby
you have at your house?"
Joan's tune may be something like this:

Joan:

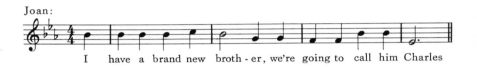

I   have a brand new broth - er, we're going to call him Charles

"Who wants to sing about something we saw at Mr.
McGrew's farm yesterday?"
Another child may sing about the farm animals:

Child:

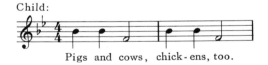

Pigs and cows, chick - ens, too.

"Who would like to sing about our bus ride out to the
farm?"
And this youngster remembers the "bumpity-bump" of the
bus.

Child:

Bump-i - ty, bump, we rode a - long, Bump-i - ty bump, we sang   a song!

2. Do simple question and answer singing.

Teacher:

What do you like   to   do   in   school ?

Child:

I   like   to   read!_____

Teacher:

I   am Miss Cart-er, Who are you?

Child:

I'm Rob-bie Ben-son, How d'you do!

3. Encourage solo singing within a song.
   One child sings one phrase; another child sings a second
   phrase; everyone sings the third and fourth phrases.
4. Encourage solo singing of an entire song.
   "Who would like to sing a song for us today?" "What
   would you like to sing?"

Many teachers give attention to individual singing in the primary
grades but seem to abandon it in the upper grades. It is essential
that this important activity continue throughout all the grades.
There is an adage, "A chorus is only as good as its individual singers."
This same philosophy can be brought down to the elementary grades
where, if individuals sing well, it follows that the entire group will
do so. The child should not lose his singing identity by hiding behind the voices of others. Some of the following devices, plus many
others, will encourage individual singing.

1. Appoint leaders for a song or a part of a song, being sure that everyone has a chance to be a leader.

    "Who will be the three leaders for our round?"

    "Tom, come up, please, and be the leader of the soprano part; Linda, you be the leader of the altos, please."

2. Encourage solo singing within the song and solo singing of the entire song.

3. Encourage individuals to add a descant or improvised harmony part to a song.

    "Bill has a good idea for a harmony part on 'London Bridge.' You sing your part, Bill, and the rest of us will hum the melody."

    "Louise and Andy are going to sing a descant for 'Swing Low, Sweet Chariot' while the rest of us sing the melody."

4. Encourage one or a few children to sing the melody while the rest of the class hums.

    "Joe, Dave, and Carol, will you sing the melody of 'All Through the Night' while the rest of us hum softly"?

IMPROVING THE SINGING VOICE

Many teachers are concerned and become discouraged when young children seem unable to sing well. The question here must be asked: What is meant by "singing well" and by what standards is the judgment made of a child's singing? It is not so much a matter of his singing well or his not singing well as the fact that he is in the process of finding his singing voice. The control of that voice is a growing, developmental process which will not mold itself into a set pattern of achievement. The zealous teacher, trying desperately to overcome "out-of-tuneness," forces her children into roles of imitation they are unable to accomplish. Judging children's voices by adult critical standards seldom brings desired results. A child will learn to sing simply by singing. If too much attention is called to too many imperfections, the joyful, spontaneous singing will cease. The child may withdraw completely and wait a long time, if ever again, to try to sing.

Some teachers still believe in grouping singers by ability, with the children who are able to sing well placed in the back of the room and those with problems in the front, the assumption being that those in front, hearing the good singing both from the rear and from the teacher standing in front of them, will be helped to find their singing voices. The teacher who is concerned about the feelings, however, of her children will not use this questionable practice. To call attention daily to a child's inadequacies is unkind, to say the least. If the real purpose of singing a song is to *enhance or to enrich a situation or a circumstance*, it becomes contradictory to have children go to their "music seats" just to sing their song. Of course, the teacher who believes in grouping by ability is not likely to be the kind who would encourage singing at any time except that which is scheduled. Consequently, to her, this would pose no problem. She wants only to teach at a given time in a given way, and becomes upset if this routine is broken.

If, by chance, all those with pitch problems are seated in the same area, there is nothing wrong with changing a place or two to gain better balance. This is especially true in part-singing.

Young children will enjoy singing while seated around a piano, at their tables, or on the floor. Older children, rather than remaining at desks or tables, sometimes enjoy grouping themselves in various ways in different parts of the room. The truth is that children are going to learn to sing no matter how or where they are seated.

Should there be drills or exercises to help the child with pitch or range problems? Not in a formal, strict kind of way. Several suggestions will be of help to the child:

1. Encourage good posture. A bodily slump automatically results in a vocal slump.

2. See that the room is ventilated.

3. Use suggestions such as:
   "Think high."
   "Come over the top."
   "Lift your voices."
   "Sing as tall as I am standing."

4. Be aware of possibilities within song material to use as aids for improved singing. If "drills" are to be used, let them emerge from the songs.

BELLS IN THE STEEPLE

Words by Eloise Williams
Swedish Melody

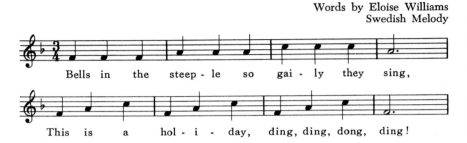

Bells in the steep - le so gai - ly they sing,

This is a hol - i - day, ding, ding, dong, ding!

From *Growing With Music,* Book 2, p. 47. © 1963 by Prentice-Hall, Inc.

a. Having sung "Bells in the Steeple," have some of the children be high bells and sing this "ding-dong."

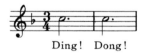

Ding! Dong!

b. "Try being this very high bell."

Ding! Dong!

c. "Now be a low-ringing bell."

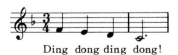

Ding dong ding dong!

(Playing these tones on resonator bells or the piano while singing, will help find the tone and maintain it.)

d. Sing another song: "Birds Are Flying Homeward."

BIRDS ARE FLYING HOMEWARD

French Folk Melody

Birds are fly - ing home - ward, Fly - ing, fly - ing,

Birds are fly - ing home - ward, Through the skies so blue,

e. "Who can be the bird in the top of the tree and sing 'way up there?"

Fly-ing up so high

f. "Someone else come flying high!"

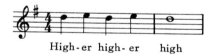

High-er high-er high

(Practically any song has rich possibilities for this kind of help.)

5. Gradually raise the pitch.

If students in the upper elementary grades have difficulty singing songs in the keys in which they are written, it is perhaps because they have never been encouraged or helped to extend their range. In a well-known song such as "America," first find the key in which it is most comfortable for them to sing. Perhaps the key is D flat:

AMERICA

My count-ry 'tis of thee, Sweet land of lib - er-ty, Of thee I sing

Raise it gradually a half step to *D,* then to *E*-flat, slowly to *E* and finally to *F.* Do this with many songs until the correct pitch can be sung comfortably.

6. Find the correct pitch for young children to sing.

In their first experiences with singing, many young children are able to sing in tune only if songs are pitched lower. By all means, in the beginning, let them sing what comes naturally and comfortably, *no matter how low it may be.* This may vary from song to song. As they gain better control of their voices, and as they become more secure in their singing, the song may gradually be pitched higher. It is better that they have the feel of the melodic contour and that they are able to sing it well in their own range than that they sing something uncomfortably or impossibly high. Doing so is one more example of the teacher getting out of the way to permit the child to learn in his own way and at his own speed. As skill is acquired and competence grows, songs may be pitched in their correct keys.

7. Give attention to tone quality.

Enthusiastic singing does not have to be equated with raucous, strident singing when there is almost always forcing, which, in turn, results in intonation problems. On the other hand, asking children to sing in a vocal whisper is almost as deplorable a practice as asking them to shout. Singing too softly results in an anemic, devitalized tone which is very uninteresting to produce and very unpleasant to hear.

BECOMING MUSICALLY LITERATE

Much has been written and spoken on the subject of learning to read music, of understanding the musical score, of learning the fundamentals of music, of developing musicality, or whatever term one prefers to use to describe musical growth. The pendulum has swung from a very formal method of note-reading to a no-fundamentals-at-all method (a "music-for-fun" kind of approach). Most music educators now believe that children should be given an opportunity to explore, understand, and use musical notation to enhance their appreciation. It is generally agreed that there may have been insufficient depth to the program heretofore, and efforts are now being made to give children a fuller, deeper, more significant understanding of music.

There was a time when note-reading was taught in a prescribed way, at a certain specified time, using specific songs and drills. A G major scale, for example, was taught at a given time, in a given grade, in a given way. Whether the children had any need for that skill at that time, or, whether any of them had had this theory before, was relatively unimportant. Such was, indeed, easy teaching, but it is doubtful if much significant learning took place.

Musical growth, to be meaningful, comes gradually. It does not take place at an exact time since it is a process of unfolding and of evolving. There is no set time and no set way in which notation should be introduced. The best time to teach any skill is when the child feels a need for the skill in order to achieve his own goals. A child may want to know why some notes are black and some are white. That is the time for some theory.

Some five-year olds were about to sing a song containing eighth notes. Their teacher asked them to look at it and then decide whether it should be fast or slow. A boy said he thought it was a fast song. When asked why, he said, "It looks so busy." That is the time to teach the concept of fast and slow. A guiding principle might be to teach each skill as early as practicable.

There is a three-fold sequence to ponder in helping children to become musically literate:

1. How does it sound?
2. How does it feel?
3. How does it look?

Another way of stating that same process is:

1. First the experience
2. Then the skill

No amount of explanation from the teacher will help the child learn that which he has not experienced. Trying mathematically to analyze the unevenly divided beat can be difficult, indeed, with young children, if they have had limited actual experience with it. On the other hand, if they have skipped and galloped and leaped so they know how it feels, if, for example, they have listened to and sung "The Battle Hymn of the Republic," seeing it and analyzing it becomes more simple and understandable. Doing something many times in many settings helps a child to comprehend. Each time there is contact with a problem, deeper understanding emerges, but the learning process cannot be hurried. A music vocabulary will be useful only if it stands for ideas already possessed.

Within the broad general framework of helping children to become musically literate are found these elements of musicianship, which must be developed:

1. Concepts of high and low (pitch)
2. Concepts of fast and slow (tempo)
3. Concepts of smoothness and unevenness (rhythm)
4. Concepts of short and long (duration)
5. Concepts of loud and soft (dynamics)
6. Concepts of happiness and sadness (mood)

With each new song that is sung, the children should be led to discover some or all of the above concepts as they occur. Thus, the specifics are taught in musical settings where they belong and not as separate items divorced from the music itself. Now, as the child looks at notation he sees not meaningless symbols but the music itself:

1. Melodic contour
    Moves up
    Moves down
    Stays in one place
2. Rhythmic tendencies
    Phrases
    Meter and pulse
    Patterns and groupings
    Accent
    Syncopation
3. Harmonic organization
    Chords
    Cadences
4. Form

    Phrases $\begin{bmatrix} \text{same} \\ \text{different} \\ \text{similar} \end{bmatrix}$

5. Expression

At this point, musical growth becomes even more sophisticated as the children feel and discover:

1. The home tone or key
2. The tonal directions or tendencies
    7 goes up to 8
    4 goes down to 3
    2 goes down to 1
    2 goes up to 3
    5 goes $\begin{bmatrix} \text{up} \\ \text{down to 1} \end{bmatrix}$
    6 goes down to 5
    1, 3, 6 are repose tones
3. The question and answer effects
    If the question phrase moves down, the answering phrase
    is likely to move up as in "White Coral Bells."

WHITE CORAL BELLS

Two-Part Song

I

White cor - al bells   up - on   a   slen - der   stalk,
Oh   don't you wish   that   you could hear them   ring?

II

Lil - ies   of   the   val - ley deck my   gar - den   walk.
That   will   hap-pen   on - ly when the   fair - ies   sing.

4. The length of tones
   The words in the song often determine the natural duration of notes.

These complexities will be understood and enjoyed only when
the child has grown into them. Attitudes and values are being developed which will last a lifetime. If too much is given too soon, the
child will lose heart and give up; however, if not enough is given,
the child is served an inadequate, impoverished musical fare, which
holds little savor for him. How a person responds in his adult life
to music is sometimes measured by the effectiveness of his musical
experience as a child.

SINGING IN HARMONY

First experiences in part singing
should be aural (by ear) ones. Children should be encouraged to
experiment with adding a harmony note or part with the advice
that if one note does not sound well, try another! One of the most
delightful experiences possible is the fellowship of group singing
with a harmony part added, producing good fun, good sounds, and
good recreation.
Try these approaches to harmony:

1. Descants
   a. Composed: "All Through the Night"

ALL THROUGH THE NIGHT

Welsh Lullaby

Ah, _____ Ah, _____

Sleep my child and peace at-tend thee, All through the night.

Ah, _____ Ah, _____

Guard-ian ang-els God will send thee, All through the night,

Ah, _____ Ah, _____

Soft the drow-sy hours are creep-ing, Hill and vale in slumb-er steep-ing,

Ah, _____ Ah, _____

I, my lov-ing vi-gil keep-ing, All through the night.

b. Improvised: "Are You Sleeping?"

ARE YOU SLEEPING?

French Folk Tune

Are you sleep - ing? Are you sleep - ing? Broth - er John?

Broth - er John? Morn-ing bells are ring - ing, Morn-ing bells are ring - ing,

Ding, Dong, Ding   Ding, Dong, Ding,

DESCANTS: ARE YOU SLEEPING?

Ring, ring, Ring, ring!   Ring, bells, ring! Ring, bells, ring!

Ring, bells, ring! Ring, bells, ring!   Wake up   ev 'ry one

(1) Everyone sings the song.
(2) Part of the group may sing the melody.
(3) Remainder of the group may sing Descant I all the way through the song while melody is being sung by first group.

(4) A two-part descant may be sung with two groups singing Descants I and II with the melody by group I.

(5) Descants III and IV may be added. Now there is a four-part descant accompanying the melody.

This same technique can be used on "Row, Row, Row Your Boat" using these descants:

DESCANTS: ROW, ROW, ROW YOUR BOAT

Row, boys, row   Row, row! row, row!   Row, row, down the stream

On "Swing Low, Sweet Chariot" these descants may be used:

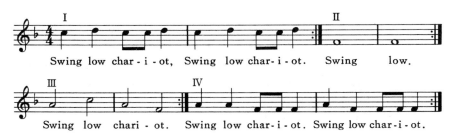

DESCANTS: SWING LOW CHARIOT

Swing low char-i-ot,   Swing low char-i-ot.   Swing   low.

Swing low chari-ot.   Swing low char-i-ot.   Swing low char-i-ot.

Descants, using tones from the tonic triad, plus some passing notes, may be used on a great many songs. Once the children catch this descanting technique, they will be eager to try some of their own ideas.

2. Rounds:

AWAKE!

German Round

A - wake, a - wake, the sun shines so bright,

The birds all are sing - ing in cheer - ful de - light.

The night, is ov - er, The sun shines so bright.

On a two-part round, the song is usually sung twice by each section. Three-part rounds are sung three times, and so forth. It is essential that the tempo be kept strict so that each section will keep together with one another. The children should sing the song well in unison before the round is attempted.

3. Combinable Songs
   a. "Shoo, Fly, Shoo!"—"Ten Little Indians"
   b. "Row, Row, Row Your Boat"—"Are You Sleeping?"—"Three Blind Mice"
   c. "There's a Long, Long Trail"—"Keep the Home Fires Burning"
   d. "Spanish Cavalier"—"My Name Is Solmon Levi"
   e. "Darling Nellie Gray"—"When You and I Were Young, Maggie"

f. "Good-night Ladies"—"When the Saints Come Marching In"
g. "All Night, All Day"—"Swing Low, Sweet Chariot"
h. "The Farmer in the Dell"—"Three Blind Mice"
i. "The Farmer in the Dell"—"Are You Sleeping?"
j. "Humoresque"—"Old Folks at Home"
k. "Ring the Banjo"—"The Girl I Left Behind Me"
l. "Silent Night"—"O Night of Holy Memory"
   Learn each song well individually before attempting
   to put them together two by two.
4. Dialogue Songs:

OL' TEXAS

Cowboy Song

I'm goin' to leave _____ ol' Tex-as now, _____ They've got no

I'm goin' to leave _____ ol' Tex-as now, _____

use _____ for the long horn cow. _____

__They've got no   use _____ for the long horn cow.__

Another example is the old English song "The Keeper."

Many songs are not planned as dialogue or antiphonal songs, but portions of them can be sung that way, as in "Bye'M Bye."

BYE'M BYE

American Folk Song

5. Singing in thirds and sixths
   a. Have everyone sing the melody of "London Bridge."
   b. Divide the class in two sections: one section sings the melody, the other section sings the harmony part a third lower all the way through until the last note, which is sung in unison:

LONDON BRIDGE

c. Try other songs using the same technique.
"Count the Stars"—harmony a third below:

COUNT THE STARS

Words by Edward J. Hermann
German Folk Melody

Smoothly

1. Count the stars so bright-ly shin - ing In the dark - ness of the
2. As the sun will rise each morn - ing, And will set at close of the

night;____ Count the sheep so calm - ly graz - ing In the
day; ____ As the waves break with - out ceas - ing, Dash - ing

ear - ly morn - ing light;____ Count the birds__ so swift - ly
rocks__ with foam - ing spray;____ As each sea - son fol - lows

fly - ing, Count the leaves__ so gent - ly fall - ing; That's how
sea - son, Af - ter win - ter comes the spring - time; Thus my

of - ten I am think - ing Of the one__ that I love best.__
love re - mains un - chang - ing; Thus my love__ to you I bring.__

From *Growing With Music,* Book 5, p. 55. © 1963 by Prentice-Hall, Inc.

"Red River Valley"—harmony mostly in thirds and sixths above:

RED RIVER VALLEY

Pioneer Song

d. Look at the notation of these and other harmony songs in music books, after learning it "by ear."

6. Vocal Chording: "Down in the Valley"

   a. Choose soloists to sing melody

   b. Divide the remainder of the class in three sections to:

      (1) Hum these chords as an accompaniment:

DOWN IN THE VALLEY

Kentucky Mountain Song

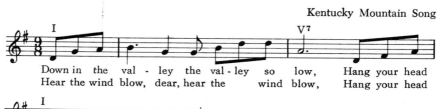

Down in the val - ley the val - ley so low,   Hang your head
Hear the wind blow, dear, hear the   wind blow,   Hang your head

ov - er   hear the wind blow.
ov - er   hear the wind blow.

I   V⁷

(Their ears will tell them to go from I to V₇ on "low"
and back to I on "blow.")

(2) Teach chords and triads, relating them to the auto
    harp and piano.

7. Adding chord tones—a sixth to the cadence of
   "Santa Lucia":

San - ta   Lu - ci - a!

a third and the root to "He's Got the Whole World in
His Hands":

He's got the whole—world—

8. Counter-melody in contrary motion: "Down in the Valley":

Counter melody

Down in the val - ley, the val - ley so low, Hang your head
Hear the wind blow, dear, Hear the wind blow, Hang your head

ov - er, hear the wind blow,
ov - er, hear the wind blow,

There cannot be too many experiences and experiments with sing-ing in harmony. It is pure joy to make and hear these pleasant sounds, besides which skill in musicianship develops when children learn to hold one part while another part is being sung. Start this process early. Let the children have *all* the music, not just the melody.

HOW TO TEACH A SONG

There is no one way to teach a song. It becomes tedious using just one method of presentation; each group responds differently. What seems to be a successful approach with one group will not necessarily be so with another. However, when a teacher wishes to teach a song, certain basic facts should be remembered, one of the important ones being that a good lesson does not just happen. Careful planning must be done. Any successful teaching situation can be only as successful as its plan-ning. Usually, the less experience a teacher has had, the more attention she needs to give to her plans. Even the experienced teacher needs to give thoughtful preparation to her teaching. Chil-dren can easily detect the unprepared teacher and may, thereby, lose respect for both the teacher and music.

Each teacher must have well-defined goals: long-range and immediate. A lesson plan should include these factors:

1. Aims and objectives
2. Materials
3. Motivation
4. Procedures
5. Evaluation

Having thus planned her lesson, the creative teacher must be flexible enough to change those plans if such a need arises. There is nothing sacred about a lesson plan.

The Unison Song
Without Books

Much song material will be taught this way. The following check-list in no way implies a step-by-step plan, but may serve as guidelines as to how to teach a song successfully.

ONCE A BIRDIE CAME FLYING

Words by Henry Winston
German Folk Tune

From *Growing With Music,* Book 1, p. 27. © 1963 by Prentice-Hall, Inc.

1. The teacher should know the song thoroughly and enjoy it herself.
2. It may be sung to the children several times in one kind of setting and then another. It may be played for them on the piano.
3. Keep the talking *about* a song to a minimum. The music will speak for itself. A few questions may be in order:

    "Does the bird fly high? How?"

    "Does he seem to be flying fast or slow?"

    "We could sing about other things which fly, couldn't we?"

    "Is this a happy-sounding song?"
4. Some of the children may want to join in the singing immediately. By all means, encourage them to do so.
5. Some background information about the song may be given.

    "This is a folk song from Germany. Who remembers what a folk song is?"

    "Carol, would you like to find Germany on our map?"
6. Hand levels may be used by the teacher to show the melodic contour and interval relationships.
7. As the children gain independence with the song, they will be able to sing much of it or all of it by themselves.

    Sometimes teachers are told they sing with the children too much, which may be true if the children become unable to sing unless the teacher sings along with them. On the other hand, it seems ridiculous for the teacher not to sing at all, if by doing so she can carry the children through a difficult passage. Moderation is the answer—too much singing or never singing with the children can both be disadvantageous.
8. If difficulties are encountered the teacher may sing that motive for the children:

    "And he perched on a tree." "Now you try it."
9. Let the children try the song by themselves. To get the proper beginning note use:

    (a) a pitch pipe giving either the key note *f* or the beginning note *a*.

(b) the auto harp or piano playing I V₇ I to establish
$$\text{F C}_7 \text{ F}$$
the feeling of and for the key.

(c) resonator bells.

(Encourage the children themselves to give these pitches)

10. Constant suggestions need to be given:

"I like the way Pattie's row is sitting!"

"Brenda, may I see your eyes?"

11. Draw ideas from the children as to what could be done with the song:

"Who would like to be the bird?"

"Can we hear birds flying? No, not usually."

"Shall we make our singing sound more like that of a bird?"

"Would it sound better faster? Let's try it!"

Part of the group may sing the story "Once a bird"—

The other half can be birds and answer: "Tra, la, la."

12. Piano or auto harp accompaniment may be added.

**Some Devices
to Make Children More
Literate Rhythmically**

These might be called rhythmic games. They obviously would not all be done at the same time. Occasionally, in place of singing a song, one or two of these will add variety and interest to a lesson:

1. Clap the rhythm while saying a child's name:
H e l-e n   H o o-v e r
Clap Clap Clap Clap

2. Draw the pattern on the board — — — —.

3. Determine what kinds of notes are represented and place them on the board: ♩ ♩ ♩ ♩

4. Discover meter signature: $\frac{4}{4}$

5. Make a game of this: "I am clapping the name of someone in our room." — — —— "Yes, it is Andy Brown. Andy, can you show us how your name looks in music?"

♩ ♩ ♩

6. Use other names—living or not living.
7. Clap the rhythm for an (a) object in the room: — — -- —

Pencil Sharpener: ♩ ♩ ♪♪♪ or, (b) something outside:

— — —— Swings and slide: ♩ ♩ ♩ or (c) a city in the

South: — — — — — — — Chattanooga, Tennessee: ♪♪♪♪♪♪

8. Clap the sound of a rhythm instrument: Drum: ♩

Using Phonograph Recordings

All of the current song book series have recorded much of their materials, which is one of the best things to have happened in music education. For the classroom teacher unable to sing adequately or accurately, these recordings are like an oasis in a desert. For everyone, they provide variety and stimulation. What teacher has at her disposal for accompanying purposes a string quartet, a pipe organ, an oboe, or a trio of brass instruments? There are, however, some obvious limitations:

A record will not teach by itself. Many of the same techniques (with the teacher using her own voice) previously mentioned should be used here.

Tempo and pitch cannot be varied.

The record and/or the record-player are not always readily available.

If the record becomes worn or the machine is not good, distortions, which defeat the purpose of using recordings, result.

A machine can never replace the teacher, nor can it be a substitute for his personality.

USING BOOKS

Primary Grades

Use song books for even the very young. They may not be able to read all of the words, but this does not matter. The earlier they see the musical score, the sooner an understanding of the symbols will result. Should syllables, numbers, or letter names be used to facilitate this understanding? If they serve as real aids to reading, they are justifiable. If they are used only as meaningless, arbitrary sounds, they serve no significant purpose. There are a number of ways to teach syllables, letters, and numbers that later may be used as crutches to facilitate understanding.

ON ST. PAUL'S STEEPLE

Traditional English

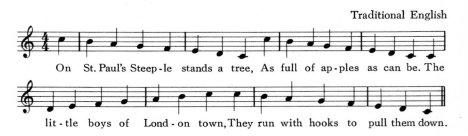

On St. Paul's Steep-le stands a tree, As full of ap-ples as can be. The lit-tle boys of Lond-on town, They run with hooks to pull them down.

1. Sing the song with words, numbers, letters, or syllables.

ON ST. PAUL'S STEEPLE

Traditional English

Do	Ti	La	So	Fa	Mi	Re	Do,	Do	Ti	La	So	Fa	Mi	Re	Do
8	7	6	5	4	3	2	1,	8	7	6	5	4	3	2	1
C	B	A	G	F	E	D	C,	C	B	A	G	F	E	D	C

Do	Re	Mi	Fa	So		La	Ti	Do,	Do		Ti	La	So	Fa		Mi	Re	Do
1	2	3	4	5		6	7	8,	8		7	6	5	4		3	2	1
C	D	E	F	G		A	B	C,	C		B	A	G	F		E	D	C

2. This may be the time to teach the scales:

   Guido D'Arrezo, an Italian, who lived from 980 to 1050, developed a system of Latin syllables used as a method to identify scale tones. Before his time there was no written musical notation. Melodies were learned by rote and passed from person to person.

   Guido adapted the first syllables of the first six lines of an old Latin hymn, each line of which started on a successively higher tone of the scale. These tones were: UT, RE, MI, FA, SO, LA. Later, "UT" was changed to "DO" and the seventh scale step "TI" was added. The ancient poem originally looked like this:

   > UTqueant laxis
   > REsonare fibris
   > MIra gestorum
   > FAmuli tuorum
   > SOluc polluti
   > LAbii reatum

3. Play the song, which consists of a complete scale, on the piano, step bells, resonator bells, or tuned water glasses.
4. Play and sing other songs with scale patterns such as "Joy to the World," noticing that the key has changed.

JOY TO THE WORLD

Music by George Frideric Handel
Words by Lowell Mason

Joyfully

Joy to the world, the Lord is come! Let earth re-
ceive her King. Let ev - ry___ heart___ pre-pare___ Him___
room,___ And heav'n and nature___ sing, And___ heav'n and nat-ure
sing, And___ heav'n and heav'n___ and na - ture sing.

"Do" and "one" will be in different places than in the last
song.

JOY TO THE WORLD

G. F. Handel

Joyfully

Do	Ti	La	So	Fa	Mi	Re	Do	So	La	La
8	7	6	5	4	3	2	1	5	6	6

Ti	Ti	Do	Do	Do	Ti	La	So	So	Fa	Mi	Do	Do	Ti	La	So
7	7	8	8	8	7	6	5	5	4	3	8	8	7	6	5

So	Fa	Mi,	Mi	Mi	Mi	Mi	Mi	Fa	So,	Fa	Mi	Re	Re	Re	Re	Mi
5	4	3	3	3	3	3	3	4	5	4	3	2	2	2	2	3

Fa	Mi	Re	Do	Do	La	So	Fa	Mi	Fa	Mi	Re	Do
4	3	2	1	8	6	5	4	3	4	3	2	1

In learning a new song, some or all of the steps listed under the following song might be followed:

MUSIC ALONE SHALL LIVE

German Melody

Mus - ic   is   ev - 'ry where   und - er   the   sun.

Though all   else   pass   a - way,   mus - ic   a - lone   shall stay,

Join   in   this   roun - de - lay,   Sing   ev - 'ry   one!

1. Discuss background of song.
2. Discover melodic tendencies:
    phrases that are alike

    motives that are alike

    the feeling of high and low

    key and beginning note
3. Discover rhythm tendencies:
    even and unevenly divided beats

    notes that move fast—notes that move slowly

    swing of 3's

    accent
4. Discuss meaning of the word, "roundelay."

5. Have a child play an *F* chord on the auto harp or an *f* or an *a* on the piano or bells.
6. *Sing the song all the way through by words.* Teacher may help if an occasional difficulty is encountered.
7. If problems are encountered with a note or two, use one of the crutches (numbers, letters, or syllables) on the troublesome note or notes.
8. Phrasing may be done: arms make a circular, "big apple" kind of motion; one of these to each phrase.

   There are other ways to phrase a song with bodily motions:

   a. Slowly extend right arm out to side on first phrase.
   b. Raise both hands above the head on first phrase, bring them back to place on second phrase, bring them slowly out in front on third phrase, and bring them back to place on fourth phrase.
   c. Bend upper torso forward on first phrase, slowly back to place on second phrase. Repeat, returning to place on fourth phrase.

   Children will have their own ideas for phrasing. Encourage them to think of other ways than these.
9. Interpret the song.

   Inner feelings, guided by the text and the music, will bring the song to life.

   Bring out the important words and musical ideas.

   The meaning of the music can be interpreted only in terms of its meaning to each individual. One child may feel one thing; another child may feel something else. Each brings to a song his background of experience, his feelings, his knowledge.

Upper Grades

There is little difference in teaching songs to older children from teaching them to young children. Any or all of the previous suggestions may be followed. The same notations have appeared again and again in a variety of settings. With each encounter the child feels a deeper understanding and a more intensive appreciation. Significant and meaningful musical growth is slowly but very surely emerging. It is still very important that every new notational problem will first have been experienced aurally before the children can solve it successfully.

In reading two-part music from the score, a rehearsal of individual parts should be used only rarely. Since the primary purpose of part-singing is to be able to sing and maintain one part while others are being sung, there is little merit, if any, in each section singing the part alone and finally bringing them together and calling that harmony. Work vertically.

HARVEST HYMN

Words by Henry Alford
Music by George J. Elvey

Come 'ye thank-ful peo-ple, come, Raise the song of har-vest home;

As in all other songs, try singing this at sight immediately. If difficulties are encountered, rather than "Sopranos, sing your part—altos, let's go over your part," approach it chord by chord:

1. Both parts sing the note for "Come."
2. *Think* how your next note sounds.
3. Both parts sing it, while listening to each other.
4. While holding that chord, *think* how "Ye" will sound.
5. Now sing it, while listening to each other.

After a few chords, the boys and girls will soon have the idea that they must keep looking ahead, *thinking* and actually *hearing* how the next chord sounds before they ever sing it.

Since few, if any, voices have changed physiologically in the primary grades, keep rotating parts. Until children gain real competence in part-singing, it is advisable to allow them to sing the same part on a given song but to change parts on the next song. There is a tendency to ask the children who are harmonically strong to sing the alto or harmony part. Let everyone have a go at it to develop power and strength.

Some educators dislike the terms soprano and alto, preferring the terms high and low instead. What they are called is not so important as how they are handled.

Some Concrete Suggestions for Teaching Notation

1. Be sure the children know what they are attempting to accomplish.
2. Establish the tonality of the song by singing or playing a chord progression in the key.
3. Sing the song first by ear; later, relate it to the score.
4. Help the children to see tonal patterns rather than separate tones.
5. Have the children clap or move to the music to establish the beat.
6. Make frequent use of accompaniments to give the full harmonic effect to the melody line.
7. Help the children analyze the music for pattern and structure, repetitions, similarities, and contrasts.
8. Encourage the children to learn about the background of the song: the composer or source, parallel listening possibilities.
9. Encourage each child to develop his own approach to music reading. Refrain from expecting the same results from everyone.
10. Recognize the importance of music reading, but do not become obsessed with it. Reading is just one facet of the program.

CREATIVE EXPERIENCES

Each child must be given many opportunities to explore and use the language of music. He should be encouraged to communicate creatively in this language so that he, personally, can express his own thoughts and feelings to provide emotional release and satisfaction. In creative music, a child may do something in his own way with little, if any, assistance from the outside. The ideas will be his own, although inspiration and encouragement may come from others. In creativity, it is important to think of the process rather than the product.

If a teacher is creative, almost always there will be creativity in her classroom. Her students will know that she has respect for their ideas even though not every suggestion from every child can be used. As each idea from each child is accepted, more ideas will be forthcoming. When a child feels secure about his own suggestions being accepted, he will be more apt to accept the ideas from other children. At this point, suggestions from the teacher may be offered to improve a child's ideas, remembering that new ways and new ideas should always be heard. In the beginning, criticism of techniques should be withheld.

The child, in this creative activity, should never have feelings of tension, nor should he be afraid to offer his musical thoughts. He should be encouraged to express his feelings freely and spontaneously, knowing that his creativity will be respected.

1. New abilities will be discovered.
2. Understandings will be realized.
3. Insights will be deepened.
4. Appreciations will be enhanced.

There will always be those in the classroom who are reluctant to offer contributions. They want to follow the more resourceful children. The shy child or one unwilling or unable to make up a tune should never be embarrassed or intimidated. In an atmosphere of creativity, free from fears and tensions, he will in his own way, at his own time, have something to contribute. When that time arrives, there will be one more happy, fulfilled child in the classroom. His first efforts may not be profound, but that is not the goal. The worth of the composition can only be measured in terms of what has happened to the child in the process.

Some or all of these ideas may be used in developing creativity:

1. Singing thoughts and ideas freely and spontaneously. (Refer to pages 17-20 for a discussion of this.)

2. Adding new words to a known song.

   To become acquainted with personnel in their building, some kindergarten children made up these words to "The Muffin Man."

DO YOU KNOW?

Traditional English Song

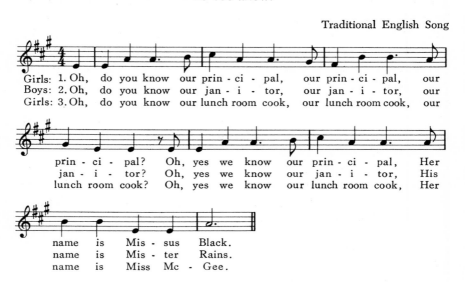

Girls: 1. Oh, do you know our prin - ci - pal, our prin - ci - pal, our
Boys: 2. Oh, do you know our jan - i - tor, our jan - i - tor, our
Girls: 3. Oh, do you know our lunch room cook, our lunch room cook, our

prin - ci - pal? Oh, yes we know our prin - ci - pal, Her
jan - i - tor? Oh, yes we know our jan - i - tor, His
lunch room cook? Oh, yes we know our lunch room cook, Her

name is Mis - sus Black.
name is Mis - ter Rains.
name is Miss Mc - Gee.

3. Making up a song.

   a. First efforts are usually in chant form. A three-year old, learning to tie his shoe laces, sang:

Tie my shoes, tie my shoes!

   b. As he continued his efforts, his song also grew:

Make a loop and tie my shoes!

c. This song emerged:

I'm a big boy now! I can tie my shoes,

Make a loop a - noth-er loop, I can tie my shoes.

d. The teacher sings a question to which a child answers (see pages 17-19).
e. One child began a musical thought:

It's time to go to lunch____

A second child added his idea:

Let's put our work a - way, ____

Then followed the next thought:

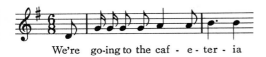

We're go-ing to the caf - e - ter - ia

The fourth child finished the song:

Don't stop a - long the way, ____

f. Setting a poem to music

A well-known poem is a good vehicle for the first attempt.

Children will write their own poem and then set it to music.

Words and music may come simultaneously.

A great deal has been written on the subject of leading children down creative paths. Authors have voluminously offered step-by-step procedures for song-writing, which should be read, evaluated, and used to whatever degree is desired. As with anything which is creative, it is difficult to decree that certain things be done in certain ways in certain sequences at certain times. The charm of creativity is spontaneity and *how* a teacher goes about encouraging creativity is perhaps not as important as *what* she is able to draw from a child. The following sugges-gestions are offered only as guidelines to assist a child in expressing himself:

(1) The poem should be read or said to the extent that the child feels the impact of it. Avoid a sing-song, unmusical style.

(2) Explore together the meaning of the words in an attempt to fuse the words and music into a musical totality. The music should give added meaning to the words and vice-versa.

What is the mood?

Where is the climax?

What should the style be?

(3) Try a variety of melodies.

Which sounds best?

Why?

(4) Experiment with rhythm patterns and tempi.

(5) Encourage unusual melodic progressions, rhythm patterns, and cadences. Some conformity is necessary, but look with favor on new ideas.

(6) In his early attempts at creativity, if a child has dif-

ficulty releasing his musical thoughts, the teacher may assist and encourage by singing a few tones or playing a I-V₇-I chord progression on the piano or auto harp.

(7) Working as a group is fine; encourage the children to "compose on their own," also.

4. Adding a harmony part to an already composed melody.
   a. Refer to pages 29-31 for suggestions.
   b. Explore such possibilities as: descants, drone bass, thirds, sixths, chromatically altered tones, discords, fifths, fourths. Again, encourage experimentation of "different" sounds.
5. Composing a simple accompaniment to a melody.
6. Inserting chord markings.
7. Notating compositions.

   Children should be encouraged to write down their musical ideas. Obviously, this cannot be done until the child knows something about theory. As a matter of fact, creative activity is often a potent motivation for a child to learn enough about theory so that he can notate his work. When he feels a need for additional knowledge about music, he is usually not only willing but eager to learn more about it.

   The classroom teacher of primary children will find it helpful if she is skilled enough to take down the tunes her children offer her. Children delight in singing over and over the songs which they have "made up." Unless a teacher has a fantastic memory, she will be unable to remember all the tunes. Moreover, the children will be delighted if they can *see* the results of their creative efforts. Many elementary teachers keep all of the songs in a large book on an easel captioned "Our Songs." Skill is necessary for notating. What is a teacher to do if she lacks such skill? These suggestions will be of help:

   a. Jot down the general melodic contour: __

   Step by step progression up __ — ‾

   Step by step progression down — __ — __

Moving in skips: large _____

Moving in skips: small ____   ____

Staying in the same place ___ ___
  b. Jot down the rhythm pattern:

Fast ___ ___ ___ ___ ___

Slow _____   _____

Combination _____   _____ ___ ___

Even and uneven _____ ___ _____ ___
  c. Ask the music teacher for assistance in the actual notation. Important as notating may be, the essence of the activity is to draw these tunes from the child. If the teacher and/or the children can notate them, fine. If not, the children will have had a meaningful experience in self-expression. In a creative atmosphere, a creative teacher will almost automatically acquire techniques for notating. Children, in such a classroom, will also become musicians skilled, at their own levels, in the craftsmanship of composition.

8. Deciding on interpretation.

9. Studying works of composers to observe their tools and methods.

10. Acquiring an appreciation for songs written by others.

11. Evaluating his own work and that of others.
    Once a child has become involved in composition and has some security in it, he can become quite objective about the worth of his work. He is ready now to welcome suggestions from his teacher and classmates:
    If it is good; why?
    If it is not good; why?
    How can this song be improved?
    How can the next attempt be better?

12. Taping Songs.
    If the song has not been notated, a tape will keep it alive. Hearing his own work brings pride and joy to the child.

He knows that he has done something, that he has said something that he can now listen to with self-respect and satisfaction.

RELATING MUSIC TO OTHER AREAS IN THE CURRICULUM

Because music is a universal language, a song can bring deeper meanings to other subjects in the curriculum. So, also, can other subjects add interest to music. As important as the correlation of one subject to another may be, however, the really vital correlation must be the child. He must be correlated with himself. His state of well-being must never be lost sight of. Because each teacher's goal is to put music into the life of each child, that goal can often be achieved when the child realizes the inter-relationships of music with other disciplines.

As in all planning, these plans also should be pupil-centered. The teacher may start things moving with a question or a comment, but then the children should take over. Once they grasp the idea that a song will enhance a story, or that a mathematical concept occurs in a certain song, or in a particular period of American history certain songs were being sung, they are on their way to correlated, integrated thinking.

Many teachers like a unit or topic approach to learning. Others prefer single, complete lessons. Whatever the plan, there should be a unifying thread weaving and interweaving within each subject and also from one subject to another. Certainly not every subject needs to integrate or correlate with every other subject, but this is a possibility, particularly with some topics or units.

The core subjects in the curriculum are social studies, language arts and science; music, art, arithmetic, health and physical education bring understandings and solutions to problems.

The following outline points out a few obvious bases for inter-relating music with other subjects in the curriculum:

1. Science
   a. Making and playing musical instruments may motivate the study of acoustics and the science of sound.

      b. Experimenting with sounds of radio, television, amplifiers, and other types of electronics.
2. Arithmetic
      a. The study of note values, beats, meter signatures relates to the understanding of number concepts.
3. Language Arts
      a. Many songs are based on literature and drama.
      b. Music, dance, and drama are communicative arts.
      c. Poetry can be compared; music can be written based on poetry.
      d. There are many books written about music, musicians, instruments.
4. Social Studies
      a. Music exemplifies man's common likenesses, understandings, ideals.
      b. Music aids in teaching history through study of appropriate music.
      c. Music helps to understand other peoples, their cultures, customs, beliefs.
5. Physical Education
      a. Basic understanding of note values and meter signatures comes from bodily response.
      b. Dances can be created to music.
6. Art
      a. Songs can be illustrated by children's drawings.
      b. Many artistic styles are common to both music and art.

The broad framework of interests from which topics will emerge begin with the child himself: his home, his neighborhood, and his school. He then looks to his community and its relationships to other communities. His horizons widen and broaden as he moves to his state, his region, his country, and finally to other countries of the world.

In a unit on "community helpers," for example, there will be stories, poetry, science, arithmetic problems, spelling words, health, art, physical education, songs, movements, films, recordings and instruments all fusing into this common topic. Some teachers are carried away by this idea and think that everything, all day, must have to do with community helpers. This could be miserably tiresome and not very meaningful. Handled wisely, it can be extremely interesting. Here are some activities that might take place:

1. A story is read about firemen
   a. Sing some firemen songs.
   b. Write a poem about firemen; set it to music.
   c. Take a field trip to the fire-house.
   d. Draw pictures of that visit.
   e. Write a thank-you note to the Fire Chief.
2. A song is sung about the bakery man.
   a. Write an original story about the baker.
   b. Relate mathematics to the song (theory).
   c. Discuss food needs in relationship to the people who provide those needs.
   d. Sing songs about other community helpers.

Possibilities are limitless. The children will volunteer many ideas. There will perhaps be too much material, too many ideas, too many activities, but deletion is easier than addition. The sensitive teacher will realize when the saturation point is near and will wisely direct the enthusiasms and energies of her children to other channels.

The following topics are of interest to children. No attempt has been made to classify them as to grade or age level. Some topics are obviously of more interest to one age than to another. Many units are of interest to any age:

1. Home and Family
2. Toys and Pets
3. Circus and Zoo
4. Carnivals
5. Animals, Birds, Insects
6. Country and Farm
     Harvests and Herds
     Tilling the Soil
     Plains
     Rivers
     Forests

7. City and Cities
8. Community Helpers
9. Clothing and Food
10. Morning and Evening
11. School and Community
12. Health and Safety
13. Seasons and Weather
14. Nature Study and Music
15. Science and Music
16. Transportation and Travel
17. Indians
18. Eskimos
19. Cowboys
20. Pioneers
21. American Negro
22. Make Believe
23. Holidays
24. Tales, Legends, Myths, Folklore
25. Territorial Expansion
26. People in Other Lands
27. Great Events and Famous Men
28. Occupations
29. Music in Early America
30. Music of Today
31. Great Composers
32. The Symphony
33. Opera
34. Music and Dance
35. Folk Songs
36. Great Paintings
37. Music Tells a Story
38. Brotherhood of Man

However important music is in a unit—and it is important—it must never be allowed to fulfill *only* that objective. Music can and does stand by itself. There is a wealth of music to be heard and sung that is not necessarily categorized in a unit. In whatever way it is approached, music must never lose its identity as music by itself and for itself.

MUSIC FOR
EXCEPTIONAL CHILDREN

There are many kinds of exceptional children encompassing an intellectual range from the mentally handicapped to the mentally gifted, from slight physical impairments to severe disturbances. Whatever such differences may be, exceptional children have much in common with their more normal classmates. One joy that all children share is their love of beautiful musical sounds.

Many exceptional children have apparent musical talents that need to be nurtured and developed. These children, because they represent a deviation from the norm, need music in their lives for enrichment and fulfillment. Through music, such a child will develop feelings of belonging, sharing, and contributing. Music will bring him something that nothing else in the curriculum can do. The very fact that a child is different means that he will inevitably have lonely hours. Here is where music—and singing specifically— can help him through those forlorn, despondent moments.

Technical musical difficulties must never stand in the way of personal satisfactions that singing a song can bring. The emphasis should not be placed on perfection of musical performance but upon the child's reaction to the activity and his involvement with the song. Music should become a living force in the life of every exceptional child. In using songs to develop a well-rounded personality, the nature of the handicap determines the approach.

1. *Blind and Partially-Sighted*

These children are particularly susceptible to music because sound and touch provide their principal contact with reality. Except where Braille is available, all songs will need to be taught by rote. Blind children, because of their acute sensitivity to sound, learn songs easily and quickly. Adding harmony parts and singing by ear come very easily to them. To increase aural perception and to develop general musicianship, several things can be done using this or any other song:

A CRADLE HYMN

Words by Isaac Watts
Music by J. S. Bach

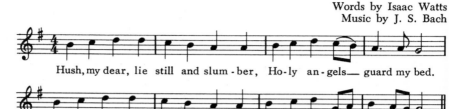

Hush, my dear, lie still and slum - ber, Ho-ly an - gels___ guard my bed.

Heav'n - ly bless-ings with-out num - ber, gent - ly fall-ing___ on thy___head

a. Teach the song to the children by rote.
b. Have them find the phrases that are exactly the same.
c. Have them identify the differences in the second and fourth phrases.
d. Let them hear that each phrase begins with the same three notes:

e. A harmony part of thirds above and/or below may be added.

A CRADLE HYMN

Words by Isaac Watts
Music by J. S. Bach

Softly

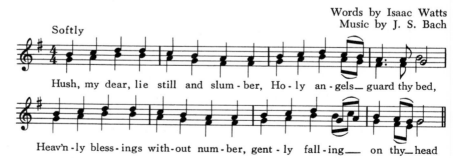

Hush, my dear, lie still and slum - ber, Ho - ly an - gels___ guard thy bed,

Heav'n - ly bless-ings with-out num - ber, gent - ly fall-ing___ on thy___head

f. The G and D₇ chords may be sung by part of the group. These same chords may be played on the piano and auto harp.

g. Tell the children something about Bach's life.

h. Play some Bach music for them on the piano or phonograph.

2. *Cerebral Palsy*

The term "cerebral palsy" implies a lack of the normal use of muscles owing to brain lesion usually occurring at birth. One or both arms or legs may be affected, as well as speech, hearing, or eyesight. Mental retardation *may* be present, but not necessarily so. Singing songs contributes greatly to speech rehabilitation. In helping the cerebral palsied learn to walk, doing so to music is very effective. Most marches are too fast to use for this purpose. This singing-game waltz can be done even by children on crutches. Help the children to sing and move slowly in time to the music.

CIRCLE AROUND

Words by Margaret Lowrey
German Folk Dance

From *Growing With Music*, Book 2, p. 17. © 1963 by Prentice-Hall, Inc.

a. Sing the song.

b. Clap and tap the accent (first beat of each measure).

c. Walk (step) on each accented beat, one step to a measure.

d. Do the simple dance as the words indicate.

3. *Deaf and Hard of Hearing*

Children with hearing problems can feel vibrations through such parts of their bodies as fingers, elbows, and feet. While deaf children can be taught to sing, greater emphasis is given to movement to music and choric speech. A deaf child's efforts to sing should never be measured by those results achieved by the child with normal hearing. Those first singing sounds made by a deaf child may be the beginning of speech rehabilitation.

4. *Mentally Retarded*

These children often possess surprising music talents. They delight in singing songs of all kinds: they often compose charming songs; they enjoy adding harmony parts and singing by ear. Some aspects of theory will be of interest to them, but there is no need to become deeply involved in music fundamenals. The slow learner may not be able to read well or spell correctly or solve complex mathematical problems, but he can sing a song in his own way and within his own limitations to bring him unsurpassed joy.

5. *Speech Problems*

To the stutterer, singing is an unexcelled pleasure because, with all of his frustrations in attempting to *speak,* he finds that, when he *sings,* these problems vanish. Sometimes this child cannot express his feelings in any way except to sing them. As the stutterer sings, tensions ease and frustrations lessen, because there is no stuttering in song.

The child who lisps is often given speech exercises to help him find the "s" and eliminate the "th" from his speech. In an exercise such as, "The slinky snake is slithering through the slough," encourage the lisper to make up a tune to that sentence to remove the drudgery and add interest or even pleasure to what might otherwise be a tiresome exercise. Something like this may emerge:

THE SNAKE

The slin - ky snake, The slin - ky snake,

Comes slith - er - ing thro' the slough.

6. *Orthopedically Handicapped*

If the impairment is great, the need to fill many hours is particularly poignant. The more songs this child can sing and the more deeply involved he can become in music, the happier his life will be. Enforced inactivity can be better endured with music.

7. *Emotionally Disturbed*

Children with emotional problems desperately need the benefits from group participation in singing and other music activities. They need the feeling of personal worth. For the seriously maladjusted child, singing a song may drain off manic actions and aggressive behavior. Often an involvement with music by the emotionally disturbed child will compensate for other lacks. Because his behavior patterns are different and he knows this, and because he is a problem to others as well as to himself, his need for music is great.

8. *The Gifted Child*

For our purposes there are three areas of giftedness in children:

a. Intellectually gifted who are also musically gifted.

b. Intellectually gifted who are not musically gifted.

c. Musically gifted who may not be intellectually gifted.

Any one of these gifted children presents a challenge to his teachers. Such a child must be motivated and guided in his intellectually oriented activities to the level of achievement to which he is capable. The gifted child differs from his more "normal" classmates in these ways:

a. Insights into meanings will be deeper.
b. Understandings will be clearer.
c. Knowledge will be more extensive.
d. Curiosity will be keener.
e. Skills will be more advanced.
f. Tastes will be determined by a discriminating judgment of values.

The gifted child will explore to the fullest all areas of music. His research will have breadth and depth. In singing and its related areas he will study:

a. The structure of the song, melody, rhythm, harmony, form, and tone color
b. Composer or source
c. Dynamic interpretation
d. Related activities:
   Listening to recordings in and out of school.
   Reading about composers and other areas of interest.
   Attending concerts, operas and professional rehearsals.
   Interviewing music personalities.
   Becoming familiar with lives and works of performing artists.
   Composing songs and accompaniments.
   Collecting and organizing materials for projects.
   Conducting experiments.
   Arranging songs.
   Serving as an assistant teacher in the classroom.
   Helping children with music problems during class and before and after school.
   Doing research.
   Finding correlative possibilities with song materials.
   Translating songs into foreign languages.
   Translating songs with foreign texts into English.
   Assisting the librarian with music materials.
   Writing program notes for school concerts.
   Preparing tape recordings of music activities.
   Learning to play instruments, particularly unusual ones, such as the Japanese koto.

Relating learnings from other academic disciplines to music and vice-versa.

Evaluating performance—his and that of others.

Specifically, gifted children can be expected to do some of the things listed following the song, "Home to Our Mountains."

HOME TO OUR MOUNTAINS "IL TROVATORE"

Verdi

a. Study melodic contour of song.
b. Analyze the rhythm, giving attention to unevenly divided beats, rests, and slurs.
c. What happens when tones are chromatically altered? Study and construct chromatic scales.
d. Study the form: phrasing, repetition, and contrast.
e. Study and construct a d-minor scale (normal (harmonic.
f. Study and construct an F-major scale.
g. Study and construct the chords in F major.
h. Play those chords on the auto harp and bells.
i. Play the chords on the piano; improvise a piano accompaniment.
j. What other terms of expression besides "Andante" could be used?
k. What is a lute?
   Report on it in class, show pictures of it.
   Bring in, if possible, a lute and other ancient instruments.
      Gather information about ancient instruments.
      Do research on instruments typical to other countries.
l. Study the life of Verdi and report on it in class.
      Write a paper on his life and works.
      Compare his style of writing with that of other composers.
m. Do research on opera:
   Where it started and when.
   Varieties.
   Composers.
   Singers and impresarios.
   Opera houses.
n. Tell the story of "Il Trovatore" to the class.
o. Help teacher find recordings; follow score while listening.
p. Invite local artists to perform portions of the opera.
q. Assist in a dramatization of "Il Trovatore" in class.
   Help design and make simple costumes.
   Speak to the physical education teacher about dances or rhythmic movement.
r. Prepare a bulletin board.
s. Study other operas of Verdi.

t. Study operas: ancient to contemporary.
u. Compose a musical dramatization based on a familiar story or on an original story.
v. Listen to radio broadcasts and telecasts of operas. Report on these.
w. If possible, attend a live performance of an opera.
x. Interview any visiting opera stars or composers.
y. Study the Italian language.
z. Relate opera to other subjects in the curriculum: English, geography, art, physical education, spelling.

Not every gifted child will have the desire, ability, or time to do all of the above things. But he should be encouraged and challenged by his teacher to go as far as he is able. There is always the danger of exploiting a gifted child to the extent that he will be resented by his classmates. The sensitive teacher will know, that above everything else, a gifted child is a human being who must not be forced into adult patterns. He has special needs that must be met and particular abilities that must be developed. The feelings which he has about music will motivate intellectual study, which, in turn, will sharpen and enhance his emotional responses.

SUMMARY

Learning is defined by educators and philosophers in a variety of ways:

Learning is growth.
Learning is development.
Learning is problem-solving.
Learning is experience.
Learning is clarification.
Learning is exploration.
Learning is experimentation.
Learning is change.

The acceptance of a definition is dependent upon the child and upon the situation. In terms of the child and his singing, whatever he learns should bring forth a change in him as an individual. While flashes of insight may come to him suddenly, learning usually results from a gradual period of exploration and then a gradual emergence of meaning.

The child should be encouraged to think of his music as a trained musician does of his. True, the child's skills are limited, but whatever he does should be in the spirit of the best he can bring to his performance, within the framework of his abilities.

Each activity and each skill should be introduced as early as possible. The danger is not so much in trying something too soon but in delaying an experience too long. Teaching must start from where the child is, then gradually but surely, must lead him from one experience to another until he accepts and even asks for the more complex. Gradually, surely, pleasantly, the child will become a musical being.

How an adult responds to music and how he feels about music almost always depends upon the kinds of musical experiences he had as a child. One of the most important legacies to pass on to children is the capacity for enjoying and understanding music.

5

The Teacher

This section should perhaps be rightfully placed at the beginning of the discussion, since the teacher is the prime factor in the entire program. The well-known spiritual could be paraphrased to say, "He's got the whole program in his hands." He must be a living example of competence, skill, dedication.

The person who teaches children through music should be aware of the power of music in the lives of boys and girls.

1. Children should be surrounded with a rich musical environment in which musical exploration and musical learning flourish.
2. The teacher can grow musically with the children, sharing experiences and feelings.
3. The teacher should be aware of unfulfilled possibilities and new vistas.
4. He must have his own stated objectives and give guidance to pupils to set up their musical goals; together they can achieve the desired results.
5. Enthusiasm and a sure knowledge that he can do something with music for children must result in a successful program.

It is the teacher's dedicated privilege and obligation to provide opportunities, materials, motivation, understanding, and stimulation. The emerging results will be positive attitudes and musical understandings.

The teacher must open doors for children, leading them into areas of new discoveries and exciting challenges. The teacher must help children add new dimensions to their lives; this involves doing things not so much *for* children but doing things *with* them. Children are curious and eager to try new experiences, but they cannot do so by themselves. Someone must help them.

Perhaps the most effective door a teacher can open for a child leads to something the teacher himself enjoys. Having opened that door, the teacher has the deep reward of seeing the flame catch hold and burn brightly. The teacher who stoops to help a child will grow tall. The child, having caught the teacher's enthusiasm and appreciation, will himself grow tall using music spontaneously and naturally in daily living.

6

The Results

Evaluation is an on-going process based essentially on stated goals. If those goals have been realistic, then they probably will have been achieved. Together with a practical realism must be some dreaming. Often, that which seems impossible does happen and dreams become a reality. It is good to aim higher than one has hopes of ever achieving.

The most profound hope a teacher has for each child is that he is a changed human being because of the songs he has sung. A teacher must ask herself these questions:

1. Does the child:
   a. sing spontaneously?
   b. ask to sing songs frequently?
   c. respond to aural beauty?
   d. become actively involved in every song?
   e. look forward to singing activities in the classroom and at assembly sings?
   f. sing his songs outside of school?

2. Has the child:
   a. developed positive and favorable attitudes toward singing?
   b. developed confidence and pleasure in using his voice?
      gained satisfaction from having mastered some skills?
      gained the ability to sing individually, in groups, in unison,
         in parts?
   c. learned to sing songs of all types?
   d. learned to listen critically to his own singing and that of
      others?
   e. developed a musical media through which he can express
      himself?
   f. developed his own critical standards of music literature and
      its performance?
   g. caught the power of music in his life?

7

Materials
and Related
Activities

BASIC MUSIC SERIES

Berg, Richard C. et al. *Music for Young Americans*. New York: American Book Company, 1959.

Ernst, Karl et al. *Birchard Music Series*. Evanston, Illinois: Summy-Birchard Co., 1962.

Landeck, Beatrice et al. *Making Music Your Own*. Morristown, New Jersey: Silver, Burdett Company, 1964.

Leonhard, Charles et al. *Discovering Music Together*. Chicago, Illinois: Follett Publishing Company.

Mursell, James L. et al. *Music for Living*. Morristown, New Jersey: Silver, Burdett Company, 1956.

Sur, William R. et al. *This Is Music*. Boston: Allyn and Bacon, Inc., 1962.

Wersen, Louis et al. *The Magic of Music*. Boston, Mass.: Ginn and Company, 1965.

Wilson, Harry R. et al. *Growing With Music*. Englewood Cliffs, N.J.: Prentice-Hall, Inc., 1963.

Wolfe, Irving et al. *Together We Sing*. Chicago, Illinois: Follett Publishing Company, 1956.

SONG COLLECTIONS

Association for Childhood Education International. *Songs Children Like.* Washington, D.C.: ACEI, 1954.

Boni, Margaret B. *The Fireside Book of Folk Songs.* New York: Simon and Schuster, Inc., 1947.

Dawley, Muriel and Roberta McLaughlin. *North American Indian Songs.* Hollywood, California: Highland Music Company, 1965.

Israel, Leo et al. *Little Folk Songs.* Delaware Water Gap, Pa.: Shawnee Press, Inc., 1963.

Krugman, Lillian D. and Alice J. Ludwig. *Little Calypsos.* New York: Carl Van Roy Co., 1955.

Landeck, Beatrice. *Songs to Grow On.* New York: Edward B. Marks Music Co., 1950.

McLaughlin, Roberta. *Folk Songs of Africa.* Hollywood, California: Highland Music Company, 1965.

McLaughlin, Roberta and Lucille Wood. *Children's Songs of Mexico.* Hollywood, California: Highland Music Company, 1965.

Perry, Sylvia and Lillian D. Krugman. *Song Tales of the West Indies.* Far Rockaway, N.Y.: Carl Van Roy Co., 1964.

White, Florence and Kazuo Akiyama. *Children's Songs from Japan.* New York: Edward B. Marks Music Corporation, 1960.

Beatrice and Max Krone have compiled and written a number of songs with descants. These range from the very easy to rather difficult. They are of all varieties and for all occasions. The publisher is Neil Kjos, Chicago.

The Cooperative Recreation Service, Delaware, Ohio has many small paperback song books in the various folk song areas.

COMMUNITY RESOURCES

Often in a community there are people from various ethnic groups and cultures. Invite them to share their songs with the children. Exchange students and teachers from other countries can open doors of unexplored delight to children.

RESEARCH, STUDY, PROFESSIONAL GROWTH

Membership in professional organizations and attendance at their meetings stimulates a teacher as few other things do. It is possible to keep abreast of publications, to see successful teachers at work, to participate in research, to enjoy fellowship with others either directly or indirectly, to hear speeches, to listen to a great deal of music, to enjoy the feeling that one is a part of something larger than himself. With an open mind, an abundance of curiosity, and a zest for new discoveries, potentialities for personal and professional growth are limitless.

UTILIZATION OF PROFESSIONAL MUSICIANS

Explore the possibility of bringing performers, composers, and scholars into the classroom for reasons other than mere entertainment. A concert singer might present a program, yes, but perhaps even more beneficial would be the actual teaching of some songs to the children. Could a contemporary composer not be commissioned to create something for children? It is being done, but not nearly to the extent it might be. Such a practice takes a child not only over the threshold, but right through the door into the very real world of music.

ELEMENTARY CHORUS

The elementary school is a place where, among other things, the child experiments with a wide range of activities. Opportunities are provided for his becoming a whole child. In music, the slogan, "music for every child, every child for music," should be given thoughtful and wholehearted application. Teachers sometimes give lip service to this philosophy and mean to put it into action, but often do not do so. The zealous teacher will dedicate her efforts to making this old slogan come true.

In so doing, the somewhat questionable practice of organizing select choruses in the elementary school is dispelled. To be sure, there are advantages for the child who is chosen to sing in such a group, but the reality must be faced of what happens to the child who is *not* chosen. If a teacher cares about children and their feelings, he will not do this to them.

A wiser approach to the setting up of a chorus is to encourage *every* child who wishes to participate to be included in the group. The child who is talented now has opportunities to express further those talents. Another child may not be especially gifted in music, but he has a strong interest in singing and, by so doing, he will develop his musical potential. A chorus thus organized can bring great benefits to the child and to the school.

There is an abundance of appropriate music available for elementary choruses. The basic song series (see p. 75) have a number of songs which may be too difficult for use in the regular classroom but which will be just right for a chorus. There are song collections and octavo numbers to fill almost any need. The goal should be the performance of quality music.

The time for chorus rehearsal depends upon individual situations. Generally speaking, these rehearsals should be held before or after school rather than asking classroom teachers to release large numbers of children during regular school hours. A music teacher who makes such demands of classroom teachers is being unrealistic and unfair.

Occasionally, when the chorus has some numbers which they enjoy doing (and are consequently doing them well), they might perform for the school or P.T.A. Public performance should be kept at a minimum, however. There will be plenty of time for this kind of activity in junior and senior high school. Motivation must go deeper than just preparing a program.

Some teachers seem to delight in organizing ensembles of one kind or another to entertain anyone who will ask them. One music teacher has a barber-shop quartet of ten and eleven-year-old boys who are on an entertainment circuit that would tax the strength of fully grown men. She has them attired in miniature barber-shop costumes, which is exploitation at its worst. Why should children be forced into adult roles so soon? There is a time for this—later. Teachers who engage in these somewhat sensational practices are usually thinking more of themselves and the satisfactions they derive from this kind of promotion.

Children should be encouraged to do their best, but to rehearse them to a level of faultless precision is questionable. A child's achievement or a group's achievement should not be measured in terms of adult standards of perfection but rather in terms of what is happening to that child.

ASSEMBLY SINGS

Bringing the entire school together frequently to sing is delightful. Being a part of such an endeavor brings great pleasure and adds new dimensions to a child's singing experiences. He enjoys his songs in the smaller, more intimate atmosphere of his own classroom, but there is unsurpassed joy in this larger enterprise. It need not always be the entire school singing; sometimes the primary rooms can gather; sometimes the upper elementary children can do so. There may be space limitations that would impose restrictions, but almost every school has a room, somewhere (even a cafeteria), where a "school sing" can be held.

Most of the time will be spent in having the entire group sing, but here is the place where an elementary chorus can sing. One "room" can sing a song for everyone else. Some schools have these assembly sings just preceding the dismissal of classes. Parents doing chauffeur duty can thus come in and join this happy closing ceremony. Perhaps there is a *Mothersingers* group in the school whom the children will enjoy hearing. Occasionally, the teachers might prepare a song or two and sing for the children. Everyone enjoys this—the children and the teachers!

What to sing? There is such an abundance of material, that this is no problem. Songs that seem to be quite difficult need not necessarily be avoided. If they are of interest to children they will learn them. Rounds and descants are very popular. Holiday songs are good. The following list may serve as a suggestion, with each teacher and school obviously wanting to add their own numbers. Bring the children into the planning of these "sings." They will have many suggestions and ideas.

SONGS FOR ASSEMBLY SINGS [1]

Elephant Song	Book 2	Page 22
Rig-a-Jig-Jig		23
Music Alone Shall Live		48
The Nut Tree		100
New River Train		124
Over the River		144
Peter Cottontail		158
We're All Together Again	Book 3	1
Goodbye Ol' Paint		16
Bicycle Built For Two		21
Pick a Bale of Cotton		29
Blue Bells of Scotland		33
The Sandman		44
Down in the Valley		49
Yankee Doodle		92
Row, Row, Row Your Boat		103
Sing Your Way Home	Book 4	3
Jacob's Ladder		12
Upward Trail		13
This Land Is Your Land		20
Marching to Pretoria		47
This Train		54
Zum Gali Gali		93
Are You Sleeping?		95
Joyful, Joyful We Adore Thee		99
Wonderful Copenhagen		128
Sing Together	Book 5	10
Cradle Song		19

[1] These songs are found in the *Growing With Music* series published by Prentice-Hall, Inc.

plus

America, America the Beautiful, Star Spangled Banner and other
patriotic songs.

PROGRAMS

Fortunately, there is now less emphasis on operetta productions and formal programs to provide entertainment for parents or to raise monies for necessary school equipment than there was once. There is little justification in disrupting children's lives and school schedules to perfect questionable productions. A program as an outgrowth of classroom activities can have real merit, but it should be child-centered. Some possibilities immediately come to mind:

1. Opera. The children may dramatize the story, singing those songs which are suitable.
2. Musical plays and stories. Having read such stories as "The

Bojabi Tree," "The Gunniwolf Story," "Three Bears," and many others, encourage the children to make up their own dramatizations and to compose their own songs.

3. Pageants. Perhaps their state is observing a centennial or their city is celebrating its birthday. Have the children gather significant data, write episodes and songs to depict historical events.

4. Unit Culminations. To climax a study of "Transportation," or "Toys and Pets," or "The Farm," or "Community Helpers," or any other unit, the children may present a program of songs and dances (preferably their own) to other classes or to the entire school.

The approach should always be one of creativity. If any costuming is to be used, nothing elaborate should even be considered, but just a touch of something to give the desired effect, which the child has designed and made should be used. Stage settings should be simple and, again, child-designed and made. Teachers and/or parents would very likely produce something more spectacular but that would contribute little to the child's growth and development. The child, properly encouraged and stimulated, can often create far beyond what a teacher thinks he can do. Their imaginations are boundless, their ability to create is limitless, if the teacher will withdraw and permit that creativity to emerge.

Children gain immeasurably in appearing before others, but adult standards are not usually acceptable. The sensitive teacher will be aware of a song or a group of songs or a program that should be shared with others, but she will not exploit her children to do so. Obviously, any sharing or performing should have some practice. But rehearsing a production to an absurd point of perfection results in loss of sparkle, spontaneity, and charm. No matter how much money has been raised, or how beautiful the costuming and lighting may be, or how perfectly the children sing, it is to no avail if something rather special has not happened to the child in the process.

Bibliography

Bibliography

Bergethon, Bjornar and Eunice Boardman. *Musical Growth in the Elementary School.* New York: Holt, Rinehart & Winston, Inc., 1963.

Coleman, Jack L. et al. *Music for Exceptional Children.* Evanston, Illinois: Summy-Birchard Co., 1964.

Ellison, Alfred. *Music with Children.* New York: McGraw-Hill Book Company, 1959.

Hartshorn, William C. et al. *Music in the Academically Talented Student in the Secondary School.* Washington, D.C.: National Education Association, 1960.

Leonhard, Charles and Robert W. House. *Foundations and Principles of Music Education.* New York: McGraw-Hill Book Company, 1959.

McMillan, L. Eileen. *Guiding Children's Growth Through Music.* Boston: Ginn and Company, 1959.

Mursell, James L. *Music Education: Principles and Programs.* Morristown, N.J.: Silver Burdett Company, 1958.

National Society for the Study of Education. *Basic Concepts in Music Education.* Chicago: University of Chicago Press, 1958.

Nye, Robert E. and Vernice T. Nye. *Music in the Elementary School,* 2nd ed. Englewood Cliffs, N.J.: Prentice-Hall, Inc., 1964.

Palisca, Claude V. *Music in Our Schools, A Search for Improvement.* Washington, D.C.: U.S. Government Printing Office, 1964.

Pierce, Anne E. *Teaching Music in the Elementary School*. New York: Holt, Rinehart & Winston, Inc., 1963.

Schubert, Inez and Lucille Wood. *The Craft of Music Teaching*. Morristown, N.J.: Silver Burdett Company, 1964.

Swanson, Bessie R. *Music in the Education of Children*. San Francisco: Wadsworth Publishing Co., 1961.

Tooze, Ruth and Beatrice Krone. *Literature and Music as Resources for Social Studies*. Englewood Cliffs, N.J.: Prentice-Hall, Inc., 1955.

Index

Index